Smart Money:

Best Tips on How to Raise Your Credit Score without Credit Repair!

Disclaimer: All photos used in this book, including the cover photo were made available under a Attribution-Non Commercial-Share Alike 2.0 Generic and sourced from Flickr

Table of content:

Introduction 4
Chapter 1: Reasons for why you need a good credit score................. 13
   Techniques to rebuild credit. 16
Chapter 2: Factors affecting your score. 19
   How to get lender offers... 22
Chapter 3: Building business credit 24
   Stop collectors fast. 27
Chapter 4: How to settle debts. 30
   Maintaining your credit. 33
Chapter 5: Fraud and identity theft prevention. 35
   Cyber Threats & Privacy... 38
Conclusion: Credit Mistakes 42

Introduction

A credit score is a number that is generated based on the analysis of a person's credit files and that represents how much creditworthiness they have. This number is gathered from credit bureaus which have created credit reports for this specific purpose. In order to create these credit reports the credit bureaus take a look at various factors and assign them values based on how much of a risk a person is to the bureau. As an example, FICO, one of the larger credit institutions, disclosed a general make up of exactly what is factored into a credit score. It should be noted that a FICO score is not the same as a credit score but rather a FICO score is a type of credit score.

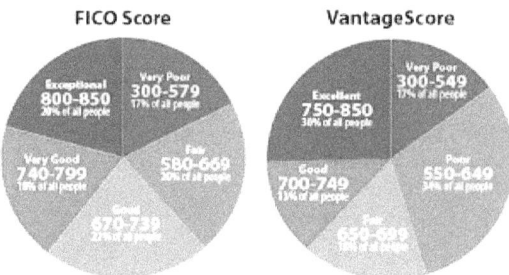

A credit score is generally composed of 10% type of credit used, 10% credit search, 15% age of credit history, 30% debt accumulation, and 35% payment history. The precise formula for a credit score is not known to the public as a rule. The components just shown are a generalization and the percentages vary with each credit institution.

This leads to a very important thing to remember when it comes to credit: there is more than one credit score since each bureau has their own credit score. The idea that there is only one universal credit score is just a product of misinformation.

There are three major credit bureaus that are responsible for compiling the credit information into credit reports that are then used for credit scores. These bureaus are Equifax, Experian, and TransUnion.

Each of the bureaus has grown to become established credit institutions in not just the United States, but around the world. Because of their wide reach the information they provide is invaluable. Lenders, consumers, employers, and all manner of financial institutions use the information that the three major bureaus supply. It is with this understanding that each of the bureaus will be looked at in detail.

The first to be discussed is TransUnion. TransUnion provides information in over 30 countries to roughly 45,000 business and 500 million consumers. These numbers are not only impressive but also make it the 3rd largest credit bureau in the United States. TransUnion formed in 1968 under the parent company of Union Tank Car Company and served the role of a holding company for the larger organization. In 1969, it became the owner of the Credit Bureau of Cook County and became responsible for maintaining almost 4 million card files. Later in 1981 the Marmon Group purchased TransUnion for $688 million. Goldman Sachs Capital Partners later purchased it in 2010. Four years after that TransUnion bought the data company TLO and in 2015 it became a publicly traded company. The years of acquiring companies and becoming acquired resulted in TransUnion becoming a business that offers predictive data that determines a consumer's ability to repay loans study debt behavior.

Experian is the second of the three big bureaus used for credit scoring. It is a global company that operates in 40 countries with the corporate headquarters located in Dublin, Ireland. Formerly known as TRW Information Services, it became the bureau that it is today through a series of business deals dating back to the 1970s. GUS plc, a retail company located in the UK, allowed for the then novel idea of letting customers purchase products on credit.

A computer programmer that worked for the company named John Peace combined all of the mail order data that the various branches of GUS utilized in order to create a central database. The database was later expanded with electoral roll data and was commercialized in 1980 under the new name of Commercial Credit Nottingham (CCN). It was then in 1996 that GUS plc purchased Experian and merged it into the CCN. This is when Experian began to broaden its range and enter new markets around the globe before separating from GUS in 2006 to once again be its own independent entity, only now it had greater resources and capital that would lead to it becoming one of the three major bureaus.

The last of the major bureaus is Equifax. Of the three it is the oldest, having first been founded as far back as 1899. It covers information for over 88 million businesses and more than 800 million consumers. Equifax was originally founded as Retail Credit Company based out of Atlanta, GA and rapidly grew as a company. By 1920 the company had spread throughout not just the United States but also Canada. Just a few decades later it had already grown to become one of the largest credit bureaus in America with files held on millions of citizens in North America.

The majority of Retail Credit Company's business came from creating reports for insurance companies when customers would apply for new policies. RCC was so efficient at this that the company became the main reporters for all of the major insurance companies.

The information that was investigated included more than just an individual's finances or health, but also a person's habits, morals, and other such statistics. This created controversy for the company during the 1960s and 1970s due to not just the information collected but also the company's willingness to sell the information to virtually anyone.

Some of the more controversial information collected included a person's marital troubles, school history, political activities, and even their sex life. Because of this the US Congress had to hold a hearing when RCC attempted to computerize its records. The hearings led to the Fair Credit Reporting Act which regulated information stored about consumers by corporations. In an effort to improve the damage caused to their company image RCC changed their name to Equifax in 1975. Under the new name the company phased out insurance reporting and focused more on credit reporting.

Together these three bureaus are the primary sources of credit reports for credit scores. Each bureau supplies its own credit report and credit score that can go on to make up an individual's entire credit history. They are not the only sources of credit services, however, as there is a financial institution that is often used in conjunction with the big three bureaus that is known is FICO.

FICO is a data analytics company focused on credit scoring. It was created in 1956 by Bill Fair and Earl Isaac. The pair met when they were both working at the Stanford Research Institute in California. The company went through a number of name changes over the years. Originally it was called Fair, Isaac and Company after the name sake of the two founders. It was then changed to Fair Isaac Corporation in 2003 before finally taking the abbreviation of FICO as the official name in 2009.

While the FICO score is the most utilized score, it is not the only score available. All credit scores that are not derived from FICO are referred to as educational credit scores. An example of an education score is VantageScore. VantageScore is a relatively newer score among the creditreporting agencies. It was created in 2006 by the three major bureaus in an attempt to compete against FICO. It is jointly owned by Equifax, Experian, and TransUnion yet it is maintained and manages as an independent company called VantageScore Solutions, LLC.

Much like FICO, VantageScore's credit scoring models uses data collected by the three major bureaus to predict the risk a potential consumer would pose and the to determine how likely they are to default on a loan. Also like FICO, VantageScore utilizes a three-digit scoring system which uses higher scores to indicate lower risks. Despite the surface level similarities between FICO and VantageScore there are some differences.

The most obvious difference is that VantageScore's design model makes it possible to be operational with all of the three bureaus' data, as opposed to FICO which has a different model for each. What this means for the consumer is that rather than having to receive credit reports and credit scores from each of the bureaus as they would with FICO, they simply require only one report and one score from VantageScore. Another difference is that how VantageScore calculates its scores. While FICO gives generalized percentages detailing how it comes to a credit score, VantageScore does not give any percentages. Instead of a number indicating the weight a credit item carries the calculations are created thusly: payment history is indicated as being extremely influential, the type and age of credit as well as the percentage of a credit limit that is used are weighted as highly influential, total debt/balance is moderately influential, lastly both recent credit and available credit are weighted as less influential.

CE Score is another different score and is published by CE Analytics. It is used by such sites as Community Empower and iQualifier.com. While it is free for consumers to obtain the score, it is distributed to 6,500 lenders throughout the Credit Plus network.

Given the amount of information that is gathered in a credit report it is important to know just how that information is used. A person's credit has an effect on several major financial activities that they would want to pursue. Some of the activities are obvious, others may be surprising.

Perhaps the most well-known affect a person's credit has is the ability to get a loan from the bank. If a person has good credit then the bank is more likely to do business with them as the credit report is an indicator of the person's ability to pay back the loan. This means that anybody looking for a loan for a home, car, or new business would have an easier time getting the bank to cooperate with them and give them a loan. On top of being more likely to receive the loan, a person with a good credit score can also expect to have a much more manageable interest rate. The bank trusts the person to make payments on time and does not expect the person to be much of a risk. The person is seen as dependable so the bank is not going to apply any pressure to ensure they are paid back.

Another obvious effect is how a person's ability to get a credit card is affected. The same rules for getting a loan from a bank apply to getting a credit card with a few differences. A person with a less than perfect credit score can still get a credit card, but there will be some restrictions in place. A person may be only to get a credit card from specific companies and with a much smaller spending limit, for example. The interest rate may also be much higher because the individual is seen as a greater risk.

The ability to rent or purchase a home is also based on a person's credit. Landlords look at a person's credit to determine if they are not only trustworthy but if they are dependable enough to pay rent on time consistently. The interest rate on a person's mortgage depends on the credit of the individual. The lower the score then the worst the interest is for the person.

Utilities are also affected by a person's credit. The utilities companies may charge extra fees or higher rates to a person with less than perfect credit. With the higher fees attached to utilities ultimately a person may have higher bills month to month. This means that instead of having a normal power bill, for example, the individual has to incur a greater fee that they otherwise would not have to pay if their credit was in a better standing.

Cellphone providers and insurance agencies may also do the same as the utilities, with the former having the ability to not just restrict the level of service a customer may receive but even outright turn down customers.

One of the more surprising impacts of a person's credit is on their romantic relationships. Studies have shown that those with good credit tend to have stronger relationships that last longer. An interesting fact that should be taken into consideration is that those of similar credit standings often end up having successful relationships as well. This is because similar credit standings, whether good or bad, can be seen as an indicator about their attitude towards money and finances. Simply put, those who have similar attitudes towards money are more likely to be compatible in other areas as well. However, it should not be ignored that 40% of adults are stated, according to these studies, as saying that knowing a person's credit score affects their desire to date that person.

This is due to the fact that when a couple is applying for a loan together, both of their credit reports are taken into consideration. If one person has great credit but the other doesn't then the lower credit score could prevent the couple from receiving the loan. This creates a feeling of being a burden on the person that has the lower credit score and can lead to hostilities.

The fact of the matter is that a good credit from one person in the couple does not cancel out the bad credit of the other person. Credit simply does not work in a way that would allow that to be case. Instead the bad credit weighs both individuals down and causes the person with good standing in their credit to incur the same penalties as the other, especially if they filed jointly for any financial endeavor. For example, if the couple were to apply for a home loan together the good credit of the one individual would not boost the standing of the other's bad credit. This is because negative and positive items in credit reports are weighted differently from each other.

As stated earlier a person's debt accounts for approximately 30% of their credit score according to FICO while something positive such as the age of a credit line accounts for only 15%. The numbers simply do not add up and this leaves the couple in a bad position to get a loan. This and other financial issues can, and often do, lead to huge strains on a couple that results in an unfortunately poor relationship.

One last major impact of a person's credit score is also a controversial one. A person's ability to get a job is often affected by their credit. While there is little direct correlation between a person's job performance and their credit history, employers still use a credit check to screen potential employees. The reasoning behind this is that employers are attempting to reduce liabilities such as theft potential and want to assess how trustworthy an employee would be if hired in to the company. Due to the lack of correlation between job performance and credit, a small number of states (including Connecticut and Illinois) have either banned or heavily restricted the practice of using a credit score to screen employees. Not every employer utilizes credit screening, but the employers most likely to do so are financial institutions and federal jobs due to the sensitive nature of their work. It should be noted that Eric Rosenberg of TransUnion who is the director of relations with state government has stated on record that no research at all shows any statistical correlation between a person's job performance, their likelihood to commit fraud against their employer, and the individual's credit report.

Taken in broader strokes the use of credit scores for anything other than determining the financial risk factor has been met with criticism. Even the case for using a credit score to analyze a person's financial risk has been called outdated and controversial. Due to this, Golden West Financial, the company that merged with Wachovia Bank, actually abandoned FICO scores all together.

Instead of relying on FICO scores they adopted a type of analysis that, while being costlier, is able to look at a potential client's employment history and assets before offering them a loan.

The last of the criticisms is that many may be inaccurately labeled as being untrustworthy and of greater risk than they actually are. What this means is that a person who by all means is financially secure may be assessed as having a lower credit score because they either self finance their expenses or because they do not have multiple credit cards. People like this would have to drastically change their financial situation in order to grow positive credit despite the fact that by any other measurement they are financially secure and not a risk.

Despite the criticisms and controversies regarding credit scores, there is simply no denying the importance credit has in a person's financial status and their ability to lead a productive life. The FICO scores, credit scores, and credit reports all serve the purpose of indicating how much a risk or liability an individual could possibly be to a given institution. Lenders and banks use these scores to determine if a person is able to get a loan or not. Employers use these scores to assess the likelihood a potential employee is going to commit any sort of fraud against them. And even personal relationships are made or broken based on the credit standing of the individuals involved. There is a very good reason why people often say that credit is more important than wealth, and these examples of just how far reaching of an effect credit can have. So, of course, the best course of action an individual can begin to take is to understand their credit as thoroughly as possible.

Chapter 1: Reasons for why you need a good credit score.

These days, society is increasingly dependent on credit scores when it comes to making a wide variety of different decisions about your future. As such, if your credit isn't as good as you might like, it will affect more than just your rates on a loan or if you are eligible for a credit card. Your credit is essentially a history that shows how strict you have been when it comes to reliably paying bills on time in the past which means a wide variety of different individuals are going to be curious about it as a way of determining how you are likely to act in the future.

Credit Score Chart

EXCELLENT 751-850
FAIR 651-750
BAD 350-650

Your credit score can vacillate from 350, indicating you are an extremely high-risk investment, to 850, which indicates anyone who loans you money is almost certain to get it back. Additionally, your credit rating is typically shown via a numerical rating from 1 (very bad) to 9 (very good). Currently only about five percent of Americans have a credit rating of 500 or lower while about fifteen percent have a score above 800 with the majority falling between the 700 and 800 range.

Living arrangements: First and foremost, your credit score affects your ability to get a mortgage and what you will pay monthly and overall. A poor credit rating can also prevent you from successfully getting a mortgage at all, or even prevent landlords from renting to you as well.

This is due to the fact that many landlords consider a lease a type of loan, after all, they are loaning you're a place to live in exchange for rent each month. If you have a low credit rating, and they do decide to rent to you, be prepared to pay extra for the privilege of having a roof over your head.

Car payments: The quality of your credit will also affect whether you will be approved for a loan for the car you are interested in purchasing as well as what your interest rate is going to be. In this case, bad credit can limit your options as fewer lenders will be willing to work with you and those that do are generally going to charge more to balance out the risk you represent. This typically translates into repayments for longer periods of time (72 months as opposed to 60 or less) and higher overall payments each month.

Job search: While the first two scenarios are to be expected, many people will be surprised to learn that a low credit score can affect your employment prospects as well. While employers can't check credit scores, they can check credit reports and many do so as a routine part of the hiring process. Depending on the job, if you have a history of poor financial responsibility an employer may be hesitant to offer you the position you have been dreaming about. Likewise, when it comes to promotions, many companies check credit reports to ensure their executives won't give the company a bad name.

Starting a business: Those who are grinding away at a 9-to-5 aren't the only ones who need to worry about their credit score, if you are self-employed a negative credit score can have even more serious implications. If you are looking to start a business with a small business loan, then you can bet lenders will check your credit score and, as most new businesses tend to fail, they will be very selective about who they lend their money to.

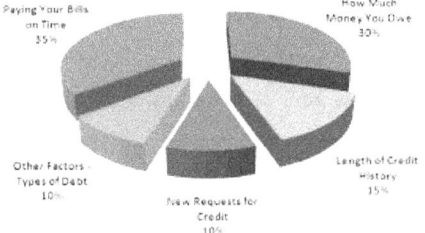

Monthly bills: Your credit score will also have an effect on many of your monthly bills including your utilities. Utility companies loan you their services every month and if your credit report shows that you are a risky investment then they will most definitely charge you more for the privilege of having electricity, running water, cellular service or cable and internet.

Techniques to rebuild credit.

Pay off what you owe: While this is going to be easier said than done in most situations, according to Experian, the ideal amount of credit utilization that you want is 30 percent or less. While there are other ways to increase your credit utilization rating, paying off what you owe on time each month will also go towards showing you can pay your bills on time, essentially pulling double duty when it comes to improving your credit score. It will also make it easier to follow through on the following tips.

Pay your credit card bills twice a month: If you have a credit card that you use on a regular basis, say for example because it offers you reward points, so much so that you max it out each month, it may actually be hurting your credit even though you pay it off in full at the end of each month.

This may be the case due to the way the credit card company reports to the credit bureau; depending on when they report each month it could show that your credit utilization rate is close to 100 percent depending on what your credit line currently is, thus hurting your credit score. As such, paying off your credit card in two smaller chunks throughout the month can actually help boost your credit without costing you anything extra overall.

Increase your credit limit: If you aren't currently in a position to pay down your credit card balance, you can still improve your credit utilization rate by increasing your current credit limit. This is an easy way to improve your credit utilization rate without putting any more money out up front. If you do this, however, it is important that you don't take advantage of the increased credit line as if you find yourself up against the limit again you will be worse off than when you started.

Only pursue this option if you have the willpower to avoid racking up extra charges, especially if you are already strapped when it comes to the payments you need to make each month; decreasing your credit utilization limit while also making more late payments is a lateral move at best.

Open a new account: Improving your credit utilization rate is one of the best ways to start rebuilding your credit. If your current credit card company won't increase your credit limit you may way to try applying for another credit card instead. If your credit is not so hot then your rates are going to be higher, but this won't matter as long as you don't plan on using the card in the first place.

Remember, credit utilization rate is a combination of your total available lines of credit so this can be a good way to drop your current utilization rate substantially, especially if you won't be able to pay off what you currently owe for a significant period of time.

Keep in mind, however, that if you choose this route then you are only going to want to apply for one new card every couple of months, especially if you aren't sure if you are going to be approved, as too many hard credit inquiries will only cause your credit score to drop, even if you do end up with a better credit utilization rate as a result. Spreading out these requests will give the inquiries time to drop off naturally and will prevent you from looking desperate to potential lenders which can also make it more difficult to get a new card.

Authorized users: If you don't have the credit to get a new credit card, or even to extend your current credit line, then your best choice may be to find someone you trust and ask them to become an authorized user on their card.

While most people will likely balk at the idea, you may be able to pacify them by explaining that you don't need a copy of their card or have any intent on using it, simply being listed on the card is enough to improve your credit utilization rating. Not only that, but you will also get credit for the on-time payments that this other person makes as well.

Chapter 2: Factors affecting your score.

There are six factors that have the most bearing on your credit score which means it will behoove you to keep an eye on all of them if you hope to retain a score as close to 850 as possible.

Credit card utilization: Your credit card utilization rate is how much credit you have available compared to how much you are currently using at any one time. It can be determined by simply dividing your credit card balances by the total limits of all of your credit cards. As such, it is beneficial to apply for a number of credit cards, even if you don't ever intend on using them. It is important to keep in mind that this amount is not calculated based on the balance that is on any one card which means you don't need to worry about maintaining a balance and rolling it over from month to month. It is always a better idea to pay off any credit card purchases as the end of the month instead.

On-time payments: Paying your bills on time is one of the easiest ways to ensure you maintain a healthy credit rating. It is weighted very heavily when it comes to influencing your credit card score which means that if you miss a few payments your score is very likely to suffer as a result.

Derogatory marks*:* Derogatory marks on your credit score include liens, foreclosures, bankruptcies and accounts that are in collections. Each of these will affect your credit rating significantly, with bankruptcies and foreclosures being the most serious. Derogatory marks will stay on your record for up to ten years and, assuming they are accurate, there is little you can do about removing them early. The average amount a derogatory mark will decrease your credit is 50 points.

The monetary amount that lead to the derogatory mark doesn't matter when it comes to your credit rating which means that have a single dollar sent to collections will still ding your credit 50 points. The date of the derogatory mark does matter, however, and it is based on when the negative action took place, not when it occurred. For example, if you defaulted on a debt in 2012 but the account wasn't sent to collections until 2017 then it will be listed as a recent derogatory mark and the seven-year timeframe will start in 2017, not 2012. Additionally, it is important to keep in mind that the derogatory mark will stay on your record regardless of whether or not you have since paid off the outstanding lien or collection amount.

Credit line age*:* The average age of your lines of credit simply refers to how long you have been building credit for. Lenders like to see that you have a long history of successfully managing credit as it makes it easier to determine if you are a risky investment or not. The longer your credit history, the more likely it is that you have been able to successfully manage your credit. As such, it is never a good idea to close out old credit card accounts, even if you don't use them anymore. Not only will this decrease your total amount of available credit, it will shrink your credit line age average as well. This doesn't just apply to credit cards but also to personal loans, student loans, auto loans and mortgages as well.

Number of accounts: As a general rule, the more lines of credit you have, the higher your credit score will be as it shows you have been given credit by more lenders. Ideally you will want to have a mix of installment and revolving credit lines for the best results. This doesn't mean you will want to go out and open as many credit cards as possible, however, as this factor weighs less heavily on your score than most.

Number of hard credit inquiries: Each time a lender checks your credit score for things like a mortgage, credit card, personal or business loan, student loan or auto loan, it will negatively affect your credit score by a few points. This effect typically wears off after a few months as long as you don't make a habit of promoting these types of checks. The effect is cumulative, however, and having multiple hard credit inquiries in a short period of time is not recommended.

How to get lender offers.

A vast majority of lenders don't have offers that are clearly defined up front, instead they have a general loan package that can be tweaked based on the situation individuals who come to them find themselves in. With this in mind, it becomes apparent why it is so important to seek out multiple offers before making a decision.

Depending on your FICO score, lenders may be more than happy to compete for your business. This fact, coupled with the lack of predetermined rates means that you can easily improve your results by shopping around and then singling out lenders who almost have the rates you are looking for and then telling them that you can get a better deal elsewhere.

To maximize this strategy, you are going to want to make a list of the features you are absolutely going to need to be happy with a given loan and then call each lender you have already talked to and go down the list point by point. If you come across a lender who has an approach that appeals to you, let the other lenders know about it and see what they can do to either match or beat it. They know they are in a competitive business and if you are willing to force their hand they will show you just how much they want your business.

Preapproved offers: If you took advantage of OptOutPrescreen.com to limit soft inquiries on your credit report and are planning on looking for lenders anytime soon then you may want to reconsider and opt back in, at least for the relatively near future. If you have not opted out of the system, and your credit isn't terrible, then putting in an application with one lender will likely trigger a barrage of competing offers from other lenders as creditors will happily provide your information to anyone and everyone who is interested in selling you on their services.

While this can be annoying in some cases, if you are looking for the best lender possible then it could be just what you need to pit several lenders against one another. Prescreened offers can make it easier for you to compare relative costs or special offers as long as you do your due diligence with each and ensure that you aren't being hornswoggled by smoke and mirrors.

Ensure you have a loan estimate document: The loan estimate document was created by the Consumer Financial Protection Bureau to make it easier for borrowers to compare the various costs associated with individual loans and lenders. Its job is to standardize and simplify the way that lenders expose their fees so that you aren't comparing apples to oranges. The loan estimate document can be downloaded from ConsumerFinance.gov.

In addition to make it easier to compare various potential loans, it makes it easy to be aware of the various fees that are sure to pile up along the way, even with the most apparently straightforward of loans. It also breaks down costs in a way that anyone can understand without the help of a CPA. It includes all sorts of useful information including estimated monthly payments, prepayment penalties and the interest rate of the various loans in question.

Lock in the best rate: Once you have done the work of comparing the various options available to you, the next thing you are going to want to do is to ensure that the best option doesn't change while you are making all of the relevant arrangements. To ensure this is the case you are going to want to ask the lender for a written rate lock or lock-in. This is a written and legally binding guarantee that the lender will give you the interest rate you discussed for the price you discussed for a set period of time. It protects you from interest rate increases that may occur while your loan is being processed. It is important to keep in mind that some lenders will charge for a lock-in while others will not it all depends on the individual lender.

Chapter 3: Building business credit

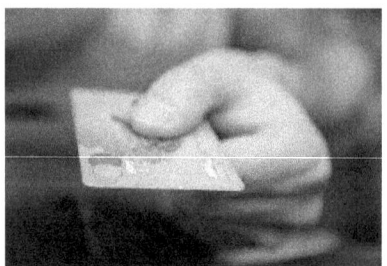

Approximately 45 percent of all small businesses who are turned down for a loan have bad credit to blame, according to the Federal Reserve Banks of Philadelphia, Cleveland, Atlanta and New York. A robust credit profile for your business doesn't just make it easier to get a loan, it will also make it easier for your business to attract new customers. This is because, unlike with your personal credit report, anyone including potential suppliers, partners and customers can all see the credit report of your business at any time. With this fact in mind, it should be clear that if you own a small business, you will want to do everything in your power to improve its credit as quickly as possible and keep it clean as well.

Know your current score: While you are already familiar with Equifax and Experian, when it comes to keeping tabs on your business credit score you are also going to need to familiarize yourself with the Dun & Bradstreet credit bureau. Unfortunately, while determining your personal credit score is relatively straightforward, all three bureaus use a different means of determining business credit scores as well as asking various lenders for differing types of data. This will sometimes work to your advantage, however as Dun & Bradstreet lets business owners update their basic business details and also upload financial data. Even better complete portfolios actually improving overall credit scores.

Set up trade lines: Assuming you purchase materials from third-party vendors, doing so in the right way can help you to improve your business' credit. Assuming you have been working with a given vendor for some time, it is likely that they would be willing to extend you trade credit for the things you purchase most often. Trade credit simply means that you will be able to pay a predetermined number of weeks, or even just days, after you have received the latest shipment of inventory. Once you set up this type of relationship it is then easy to ask the supplier to report your payments to the relevant credit bureaus.

You will want to try your hardest to establish at least three of these types of relationships as doing so will allow you to get what is known as a Paydex score through Dun & Bradstreet which is a measure of your successful payment history. Even if you form relationships with smaller vendors who don't typically report details, by listing them on your account as trade references the bureau will then follow up with them to generate your score.

Be prompt with payments: Just like with your personal finances, paying creditors on time is a crucial part of building your business credit successfully. If you are looking to get the best Paydex score from Dun & Bradstreet you are going to need to go above and beyond and make all your payments early, no exceptions. Additionally, the longer your credit history the better so the sooner you can start forming these relationships the better it will be for your score.

Borrow from the right lenders: While having a loan and paying it on time can help to boost your business' credit score, this will only be the case if the lender you choose reports to the bureaus which is far from guaranteed. Do your homework and make sure that your fiscal responsibility is helping you out as much as possible when you do get a loan. Most banks will report to the bureaus as do the online lenders including BlueVine, Kabbage, Funding Circle Fundation,

Lending Club and OnDeck. Fundbox, Lighter Captial, SmarBiz and most merchant cash advance companies do not. If you are using business credit cards, strive to keep your credit utilization under 20 percent for the best results.

Be aware of your public records: Just like your business credit report, your public records can also be seen by anyone which means you are going to want to do your best to stay on the right side the law. Not only will negative public records affect your business credit score, they will affect the way the public perceives your business as well.

Stop collectors fast.

While it is always going to be a better choice to deal with creditors directly rather than waiting for a debt to reach collections, if it does reach this point it is important to keep in mind that you still have options thanks to what is known as the Fair Debt Collection Practices act.

Ask for details in writing: Within 5 days of making contact, a debt collector is obligated to send you a written notice outlining the amount of money you owe, who you owe it to and how to dispute the claim. Most debt collectors won't do this automatically, however which means the first contact you have with them should include asking for this information and nothing else. The goal of the debt collector is to force you to confirm that you will pay the debt or make a payment, and not having all of the details in front of you can make it easy to say the wrong thing and wave many of your rights without even realizing it. What's more, asking for a copy of the details will prevent them from contacting you again until you have received them, giving you some time to get your defenses together if you have been caught off guard.

Dispute the claim: Once you have received the details of the claim in writing, the next thing you are going to want to do is to dispute the claim using the methods discussed in previous chapters, regardless of whether or not you believe you owe the money in question. This will put the onus on the collection agency to verify the debt, which is far from a sure thing even on debts that you do owe. You have 30 days to send this letter from the date you received the details which means that using certified mail is key. Be sure to ask for a delivery receipt as nine times out of ten the collections agency will deny they received your request. Once you send this letter and notify the collection agency of this fact, they cannot contact you again until the debt has been verified. **They also have to stop all reporting activity, make sure you demand this in the letter.**

Keep track of everything: As discussed previously, debt collectors are limited in how they can approach you but, in most cases, will try and skirt these restrictions as much as possible in an effort to get you to agree to pay the debt or set up a payment plan. As such, it is in your best interest to take detailed notes every time you speak with them and keep anything they send you so you can look it over for violations at a later date.

Illegal activities not previously covered include speaking to anyone but you or your representation about the debt, using abusive language, misrepresenting the amount of the debt of making false claims about legal action, seizing property or garnishing wages if they don't intend to actually follow through. If they do any of these things, then the issue of the amount of debt you owe will essentially become moot as you will be able to take legal action against them and even the threat of doing so will often be enough for them to forgive some or all of your debt entirely. Be sure not to mention that you are keeping track of your conversations as this will cause them to be on their best behavior and decrease your potential for leverage.

Speak as little as possible: Everything that a debt collector says is for the purpose of collecting on the debt which means that the less you say, the less they have to use against you. Remember, regardless of what they may say up front, they are never really your friend, nor do they have your best interests at heart. They work on commission which means the more they get from you the more they will make. Never commit to anything, never agree that you owe the amount in question, always mention that you are considering bankruptcy and discuss payment options only if you intend to follow through. If they determine that you are unlikely to pay, and the amount owed is less than $2,500, they may give up and consider you more trouble than you are worth. While the debt will remain on your credit report for the next seven years, it might be worth it, depending on your current financial situation.

Be aware of time limits: Once you receive the details from the collection agency, you will need to look into the timeframe which they have to collect on the debt based on where you live (between three and six years in most cases). Once this period of time has passed they can no longer take legal action against you. It is important to be aware of these limits as if you make a payment after this period of time, some states will allow the clock to be reset, the same can be said for acknowledging you owe the debt or for signing up for a repayment plan.

Chapter 4: How to settle debts.

While creditors would like you to think otherwise, the fact of the matter is that any debt that you have is negotiable. What's more, regardless of the amount, 90 percent of creditors are going to be willing to take a lump sum now over a promise to pay at a later date. When it comes to negotiating large amounts, the following tips may make it easier to come out ahead.

Have a story and stick with it: The person you are dealing with isn't going to be interested in your life story, but they will need to know why you are unable to pay in full right now. This means you are going to want to have a story that outlines your hardships and explains what you are doing to get back on track. You will want to distill that story down to the most important points and never waver from it throughout the negotiation process.

One particularly useful strategy is mentioning that, due to financial hardship, you will soon be meeting with a lawyer who specializes in bankruptcy. This will almost always make creditors more willing to strike a deal as if you file for bankruptcy there is a chance that they will get nothing.

Stay calm: It is important to keep in mind that, no matter what the creditor says, you have the upper hand as the debt you have is leverage over them. Stick to this fact and, no matter what they say, do your best to avoid losing your temper. If you make a scene or cause drama then the creditor will know they are getting to you and will be less willing to make a deal. If you feel yourself losing it, simply tell them that you will call them back and end the call as quickly as possible. If you find the creditor's behavior hard to stomach, simply tell them you are recording the conversation which will put them on their best, and most professional, behavior.

Always ask questions: If the creditor threatens you with a lawsuit or with the loss of property, above all else it is important that you don't let these threats frighten you into making a poor decision. Instead, it is important to ask questions as this will often reveal if the creditor is bluffing or not. For example, if they threaten you with a lawsuit, simply ask when you can expect to be notified of it. Keep notes of these threats as they are often times illegal as creditors are strictly limited as to how they can approach debt, specifically to protect consumers.

Likewise, you are going to want to take notes every time you speak with a creditor including the name of the person you spoke with, the date and the things that were discussed, especially threats. There is typically a statute of limitations as to how long the creditor has to collect on a debt, which varies by region, and they will likely become irater as that time period approaches.

Avoid agreeing to a payment plan: If you agree to a payment plan you will always end up paying more in the long run then if you manage to scrape together a lump sum payment. Depending on the amount you owe, even as little as 30 percent might be enough to satisfy the creditor assuming it is getting close to the end of the timeframe they have to collect on the debt and you have stuck to your story about financial hardship and bankruptcy.

Never be afraid to offer a lowball number, the worst that can happen is that they refuse to take it. If you do end up agreeing to a payment plan make sure you go over your expenses with a fine-tooth comb and ensure you can afford to make the payment every month to avoid finding yourself back in the same situation.

Try and deal with creditors: If you know you are going to be unable to make payments on a debt you have accrued, do your best to come to an agreement with the creditor directly, before the debt is sent to collections. The creditor is always going to be easier to negotiate with than a third-party debt collection service.

Maintaining your credit.

Once you have done the work of repairing your damaged credit score you are going to want to do everything in your power in order to ensure that you don't find yourself back where you started. You have worked diligently to repair the mistakes of the past; don't use it as an excuse to start making new ones. To help keep you on the straight and narrow, consider the following tips.

Always pay your bills on time, all of them: While not every bill that you have will end up on your credit report if you are a few days late when it comes to paying it, you can never know for certain which bills are mission critical and which can be safely ignored until your next pay check. Even a small fine from the local library could ultimately end up on your credit report, dinging your hard-won credit score in the process. Don't take that chance and always remain vigilant when it comes to paying your bills on time.

Avoid using credit cards: While having credit cards improves your credit utilization and credit history, using them too often is a surefire way to start backsliding, especially if your budget is on the lean side. If you must use your credit cards, take special care to ensure that you never exceed a credit utilization of 30 percent as that's when your credit score will start to take a hit. While going over this limit slightly will only affect your score by a few points, if you are just on the edge of an acceptable score, that might be all it takes to start seeing higher rates as a result.

Pay down your loans: Once you have righted your financial ship, the best way you can keep it on course is to make it a point of paying down your loans as quickly as possible; don't forget, approximately 30 percent of your credit score is influenced by the amount of debt you have which makes it one of the easiest ways to continue improving your score once you are moving in the right direction.

In order to make more money available to pay down your debt, the first thing you are going to want to do is to stop living paycheck to paycheck which means establishing an emergency fund. A solid emergency fund will allow you to live for three months, and pay all your bills, if the worst happens and you find yourself out of the job. Establishing this fund will give you the wiggle room you need to prioritize your debt without worrying about every minor pitfall that comes your way.

Monitor spending: Approximately 40 percent of individuals who find themselves with credit score issues got there simply by not keeping track of their week-to-week spending as well as they should. With the prevalence of online banking, there is no reason why you shouldn't be aware of exactly what your checking account balance is, every minute of every day. Get in the habit of monitoring your spending and you will never be surprised when your bank statement shows up at the end of the month. This doesn't mean you won't want to peruse the statement when it does come in, however, as you never know when a mistake might be made, you never know when a little extra diligence could pay off in a big way.

Remain glued to your credit report: Just because you are out of the woods doesn't mean that nothing new is going to show up on your credit report, whether it is your fault or not. Something new from your past might show up, or one of the bureaus may make a mistake or fail to note the positive changes you have made in a timely manner. The previous chapters have given you tools for dealing with these issues, but you will only be able to put them into action if you are aware of them in the first place. Don't let all your hard work go to waste, continue taking advantage of your free credit report every year.

Chapter 5: Fraud and identity theft prevention.

Once you have established a quality credit score, you need to do your best to protect it by taking extra steps to prevent identity theft and other types of fraud. The following tips will help you do so:

Respond to voicemail intelligently: If you receive a voicemail from someone claiming to be from your credit card company or bank, only respond by calling back the number that is printed on your card. This is the only number you can guarantee won't lead to a fraud scenario. The same goes for emails, even if they appear to be legitimate, you should only ever contact your bank or credit card company through obviously official channels that you instigate to ensure they are legitimate.

Take extra care with signatures: Not many people are aware, but you can actually sign your credit and debit cards with the phrase "see identification". While this will force you to show your ID much more frequently, it will also prevent anyone who is attempting to use it illegally from being able to do so. Unless they have a fake ID with your name and accurate signature they will be out of luck.

Be frugal with your credit card number: Ninety percent of the time any website that asks for your credit or debit card number "for identification purposes" has only dubious intentions in mind. Unless you are planning on buying something from the site you are going to want to avoid providing this information. The fewer places that your personal details are available online the less risk you run of falling victim to fraud.

Be diligent about your privacy: Even if you have already set them to the max settings, it is important to check both your browser and social media settings on a regular basis to ensure they are as you left them. You never know when an update could have come along and reset them or changed something else that affected them in some way. It only takes one slip to allow someone with malicious intent through, which is why it pays to stay vigilant. Likewise, every time you visit a secure website, take an extra moment to clear your browser's cache and history to prevent anyone from tracking down personal information that way.

Unsubscribe sparingly: If you receive an email newsletter and you aren't sure where it came from, never click the unsubscribe button. This will let the spammer know that they have a live email address and they will redouble their efforts, at best, or initiate additional tactics to procure your private data now that they have your email address, at worst. Even if the spammer has no ulterior motives than to get you to read their newsletter you are always better off just hitting the spam button and forgetting about it.

Be aware of online store security: When you are shopping online be sure to make a point of never entering sensitive information if the website isn't secure. You can determine if a site is using a secure connection if the web address starts with http**s** or if it features a padlock icon in the top right corner. Either of these are an indicator that the website is encrypted which will make it much more difficult for fraud to occur based on the transaction. Entering your details via a standard http connection is little more than asking for trouble.

Have varying passwords: In addition to the obvious, such as not using birthdays or loved ones' names as passwords, it is important to have varying levels of password security for the most secure results.

You are going to want to have at least one password for low-security sites that you aren't terribly worried about being hacked, a more secure password for online stores and the like and a separate password entirely when it comes to banks or credit card websites that are more complicated still. You should never store your passwords anywhere on your computer or anywhere in real life where other people, with potentially malicious intent, are likely to have access to and, if you must write them down, don't keep them near your computer.

Cyber Threats & Privacy

Identity theft and hacking are growing at super exponential rates. It won't stop and will only get worse. The fact is that most Americans are already compromised and they don't even know it. It is estimated that over 80% of all residential households in American do not even have their WiFi router secured properly.

Wireless Card Scanners

These are hackers that will scan your credit card in your pocket at coffee shops or other unassuming public places. They have special devices or programs that can "see" the RF chips embedded in your credit card on their laptops. This happened to me once but since I was set up on **banking text alerts** I was able to stop it and get my money back. I now use radio frequency shield card slots and wallets to prevent this from happening again, which you can buy on Amazon.

Online Banking

Make sure your network is secure and the browser is set to HTTPS when logging into your banking account. One small compromise and someone can steal your info, and ruin your credit. In fact any website you submit personal info on should start with HTTPS (Secure) URL.

In addition, over 80% of all U.S. homes do not secure their wifi router. Most people never change their factory default router login and password. Any hacker that scans your neighborhood (and yes they still do this) can generally determine what kind of router model you have from the SSID default broadcast, and then check to see if they can login using the default pass and username.

If a hacker is able to break into your home network, you can have some serious compromises. This often leads to cases of identity theft and fraud. Most often you will not know about it until well after the compromise has occurred and someone has used your information to steal money or your identity.

The cyber threats are VERY real and much worse than you think; they are only getting more complex everyday as hackers develop new technologies and methods to scan for weaknesses and infiltrate unassuming homes, people and businesses.

Shred your mail, bills or paperwork that may have sensitive personal info on them. You would be surprised to know that people still rummage through garbage to find data to sell or use for gain.

Use Secured Email

Almost everyone sends sensitive info via email and text not even thinking that someone can scan that data in "cyberspace" if they are looking for it. Since most people are now using Gmail,Yahoo Hotmail, *etc*. There aren't very many secure options for email if you are not using Thunderbird or Outlook. **However, there is one company in Switzerland that has a service called ProtonMail.com.**

It a browser email account with mobile phone apps that send and received encrypted mail and is very easy to use. They have a free account version and a paid account version, which is approximately $6 per month. If you send personal data via email such as tax returns, social security numbers, credit card numbers… Check out ProtonMail.com

Commercial Mailbox

Use a commercial mail box, such as the UPS store mail box, for receiving your postal mail instead of receiving it at home. UPS Stores are very flexible and can even forward your mail wherever you are. Many thieves still steal mail in an attempt to find social security numbers, checks, or anything they can use to extract money or credit from a victim

Conclusion: Credit Mistakes

When it comes to credit reports there is one thing that should be taken into consideration. What should be understood is that mistakes happen. These mistakes are not "mistakes" in the sense of some irresponsible action on the part of the consumer or anything of a similar nature. Instead these mistakes are actually errors that appear on a credit report. The erroneous information on the credit report could be reported incorrectly, belong to some other person, or even be against the law.

The fact that these errors can occur is a reason why it is important for a person to check their credit report. According to the Federal Trade Commission 25% of Americans have at least one major error in their credit reports. These errors are causing the millions of people to have worse credit than they actually have, which means that they are paying more for things that they are supposed to pay. This causes the snowball effect where they incur more debts, higher fees, and even loss of financial opportunities all through no fault of their own. In short, credit mistakes are dangerous.

In order to avoid the path of financial danger a person should carefully look over their credit report to spot errors that could actually be hurting their credit. Thankfully many of the errors are easy to spot and can be reported in order to repair the damage done. The most common credit report errors fall under three categories: personal information errors, account related errors, and derogatory mark errors.

Derogatory marks are long lasting negative records on a credit report. These marks generally last for at least 7 years on a credit report and have a huge ability to hurt a person's credit. Bankruptcy, tax liens, collections, and foreclosures are examples of derogatory marks. Because of the severity of damage derogatory marks can cause errors of this sort are especially dangerous.

There are a few key things to look for when it comes to derogatory mark errors. One such error to be wary of is a collections account that has been paid off still remaining on the credit report as unpaid. This is an obvious error that is easy to dispute. There will be documentation showing that the account has been paid and contacting the creditor directly often leads to satisfactory results in getting the issue resolved.

Another common derogatory mark error is a paid tax lien that has remained on a credit report for more than 7 years after the last date of payment. While an unpaid tax lien may stay on a credit report indefinitely, there is simply no reason for a tax lien that has been paid to remain after 7 years. It is a black mark on a credit report that does not need to exist.

A discharged account displayed as an active balance is also a key error to keep an eye on. This is perhaps the most damaging of derogatory marks because it concerns bankruptcy. A person files for bankruptcy as a last resort in order to gain some relief from debt obligations.

The individual has entered into a legal process in an attempt to address overwhelming debt. Bankruptcy changes the accounts a person holds and the person no longer has the same active balances they had before filing for bankruptcy. Therefore, when a discharged account appears on a credit report as active what this does to a person's credit is damage it even further than is legally allowed. The bankrupt accounts are already in a special legal process to prevent further debts and that means it is close to impossible to actually have an active account with a balance.

These derogatory mark errors should be immediately disputed in order to prevent any further damage to one's credit. While all credit errors should be disputed, it is the derogatory marks that are the most damaging due to the sheer amount of time they remain on a credit report and the severity of the impact they can incur on an individual. A person that erroneously has an unpaid tax lien on their credit report could potentially be feeling the financial effect of that mistake for life simply because they didn't look at their credit report and dispute the mistake. The other common types of errors should not be discounted however.

Account related errors are mistakes that occur which are still damaging but not to the same severity as derogatory marks. These are errors tend to be simple fixes that take little effort to correct and probably only occur as an oversight.

An example of an account related error is a late payment that has remained on the credit report after 7 years. Generally, a credit report only lists negative information on an account for 7 years, after which it is removed from the credit report. It should be noted that the debt negative items cause still exist and still impact a person's credit. However, after the allotted time they can no longer incur more of an effect, in other words the 7-year mark is the ceiling for damage to a credit report. When a late payment remains on a credit report after this time that means it is still causing a negative impact on a person's credit. This should not appear on a credit report and should be disputed.

Another common account related error is one that is more the result of simple human error, however it could still have a negative impact if left undisputed. A loan or credit card listed on a credit report that does not belong to the individual is an error that happens on a regular basis. There could be any number of reasons for these to appear but usually it is the result of a person that had a simple mix-up while entering data. The worst-case scenario is actually a more frightening occurrence because the erroneous accounts could be the result of fraud or identity theft.

The first thing to do in either scenario is for the individual to report the false accounts directly to the credit bureau which lists the accounts. This can be done by mail, fax, email, or over the phone. It is quicker to do it by phone however disputing the account by mail provides a paper trail that can be used to support the claim that the person is actively trying to dispute the false accounts. Whichever method is chosen the following step should be to close the damaging account to prevent any future harm. Thankfully the process of fixing this error often proves successful and the fraudulent or erroneous account will be removed efficiently from the credit report.

The final category of credit mistakes is erroneous personal information. This category is the least damaging of mistakes but still has an effect on a person's credit. Like account related errors, these mistakes can often simply be attributed to human error. Thankfully personal information mistakes are the easiest to fix due to them not being directly related to financial actions.

The most common error when it comes to personal information is simply having the wrong name listed. This could be as harmless as spelling a person's name incorrectly or using an individual's maiden name after they've married. Another common error is a wrong mailing address listed on a credit report.

Perhaps a person with a similar name lived at the mistaken address and whomever is responsible for correcting that information simply overlooked it. This could also happen when a person's employer information is displayed inaccurately on a credit report, a person with a similar name may have been employed by the mistaken employer.

Generally, mistakes in personal information have little to no effect on an individual's credit score. Unless the error is related to something along the lines of fraud or identity theft then there is no reason to be worried. Simply reporting to the creditors the mistake in personal information is enough to fix the problem and no harm would be done to the person's credit.

When these mistakes are made they can be removed from a person's credit report. These items are also automatically removed after the regulatory 7 years have passed, generally. However, it is also possible to remove all negative items from a credit report. The process is not difficult and can go a long way towards improving a person's credit standing.

One of the most surprising and efficient ways to remove a negative item such as a late payment is to write a letter. Often called a goodwill letter or goodwill adjustment, a person can write (or call, although writing is better) to a creditor to get a late payment forgiven and thus removed from a credit report. This tends to work best if a person has a good history with the creditor as that makes them more likely to forgive the late payment as a one-time issue.

When contacting the creditor a few key things must be discussed with them for the best results. First of all, an explanation is owed to the creditor for the late payment. Telling the creditor the financial situation that led to the payment being late could generate some understanding and sympathy.

People are not perfect and unexpected events do occur, after all. Creditors are not machines but are institutions ran by people who can relate to what another person is going through.

What should also be discussed with the creditor is an explanation of the history with the creditor. A person that reminds the creditor that they have been in great standing with no issue can reinforce the fact that the late payment was not a regular occurrence. Requesting the removal of the negative mark should be made only after it has been established that there will be no repeat of late payments.

This tactic of writing the creditor to remove the late payment from a credit report is often more successful than people would imagine. Creditors are always willing to negotiate with people because they want their business. It should be noted that writing the creditor to request the removal of a late payment only works for those who are in good standing with the creditor. A person with a history of late payments is far less likely to get a sympathetic response as they have not shown that they are trust worthy. However even in that scenario it is still very likely that the creditor would be willing to negotiate a payment plan at the very least.

Regardless of the one's standing with a creditor it is always a helpful and beneficial plan to contact them. If a person is not able to remove the negative marks from their credit report then they are still going to be able to discuss options that will lead to positive impacts to a credit score in the future.

That is the biggest secret to getting negative items removed from a credit report, simply contacting the creditor. Many people are afraid of doing so because they feel that it would be difficult or they simply want to avoid the confrontation, but it cannot be stressed enough that a creditor is always willing to negotiate. Combining this with the fact that the passage of time can generally takes care of negative marks on a credit report and that leaves a clean credit report.

In conjunction with a person checking their credit report for mistakes and monitoring changes results in a credit report that will remain free of negative marks for as long as the individual continues to be responsible.

Credit mistakes are common, that much is clear. With the proper tools and understanding is far easier than people realize to fix these errors, especially since these errors are not the result of negligent or poor behavior on the part of the individual but rather that of the financial institutions, creditors, and bureaus. Mistakes happen, that much is unavoidable. What should be done to fix these mistakes, regardless of who is at fault, is swift and steady action on the part of the wronged person. There is simply no reason or benefit to walking around with a debt on a person's record that should not be there. Nor is there any reason to ignore their credit report and the mistakes listed on them. Vigilance is a requirement in order to make sure one's credit standing is as accurate as possible. Bureaus and other financial institutions are run by humans, not machines, so mistakes should be expected. Again, staying vigilant is the key.